WILD AGE

ICE AGE GIANTS

STEVE PARKER

QEB

QEB Publishing

Project Editor: Carey Scott
Designer: Stefan Morris Design
Illustrations: The Art Agency and MW Digital Graphics
Picture Researcher: Maria Joannou

Library of Congress Cataloging-in-Publication Data
Parker, Steve, 1952-
  Ice age roamers / Steve Parker.
     p. cm. -- (QEB wild age)
  Includes index.
  ISBN 978-1-59566-911-7 (lib. bdg.)
  1. Paleontology--Pleistocene--Juvenile literature. 2. Glacial
epoch--Juvenile literature. 3. Mammals, Fossil--Juvenile literature. I.
Title.
  QE697.P365 2011
  569--dc22
2010001152

Printed in China

Copyright © QEB Publishing,
Inc. 2010

Published in the United States
by
QEB Publishing, Inc.
3 Wrigley, Suite A
Irvine, CA 92618

www.qed-publishing.co.uk

Picture credits

Key: t=top, b=bottom, r=right, l=left, c=centre
Alamy Images Martin Arpon 16b, 29tl; Bridgeman Art Library Private Collection/©Look and
Learn 17, 28tr; Corbis Bettmann 26; DK Images Peter Visscher 4br, Jon Hughes/Bedrock Studios
5bl, 8-9, 14-15, 15b, 28cl (hipparion), 29cl (dire wolf), 30cr (woolly mammoth), Demetrio Carrasco
13r, 28br, Bedrock Studios 20-21, 29cr (giant wombat), Peter Bull 29tr; FLPA Philip Perry 4-5t,
28tl; Istockphoto Dawn Hagan 3b, Breckeni 5br; Photolibrary De Agostini Editore 4bl, 4bl (plant),
9t, 11t, 22-23t, 28cr (megantereon), 30tl, 30tr, 30cr (woolly rhino); Science Photo Library Herve
Conge, ISM 5tr, Mauricio Anton 6-7, 27, 28bl, 30bl, 30br, Jaime Chirinos 21t, 29cl (marsupial lion),
Tom McHugh 22-23b, 29bl, Julie Dermansky 25b, 28cr (American mastodon); Shutterstock Jim
Barber 2t, Steve Collender 2b, Ryan M. Bolton 3t, M. Dykstra 4br (cockroach); Stock
Exchange 1; The Art Agency Myke Taylor, 10-11, 12-13, 18, 18-19, 24-25, 28cl
(pygmy teloceras), 29cr (cave bear), 29br, 30cl (giant deer),
30cl (Columbian mammoth) All maps: Mark
Walker MW Digital Graphics

The words in **bold** are
explained in the Glossary
on page 31.

CONTENTS

MANY ICE AGES

Have you been to a cold, snowy, icy place? Imagine living there all the time. You would be freezing! That's what huge parts of our world were like long, long ago—yet animals survived.

Today there is plenty of snow and ice around the **North and South Poles**. In a real Ice Age, much larger areas of the Earth were frozen over for thousands or even millions of years. This has happened many times since the Earth began.

One of the coldest times was the Andean-Saharan Ice Age, which started about 460 million years ago. Up to half the world was frozen for more than 20 million years. It was the time of **Snowball Earth**. Even in the warmer places, creatures and plants struggled to survive.

Andean-Saharan Ice Age **460–430 mya**

Karoo Ice Age **350–270 mya**

Ediacaran	Cambrian	Ordovician	Silurian	Devonian	Carboniferous	Permian
before 542 mya	542–488 mya	488–444 mya	444–416 mya	416–359 mya	359–299 mya	299–251 mya

550 mya   500 mya   400 mya   300 mya

540 mya   460 mya   430 mya   360 mya

Shelled sea animals   Land plants   Tiny land animals   Four-legged land animals

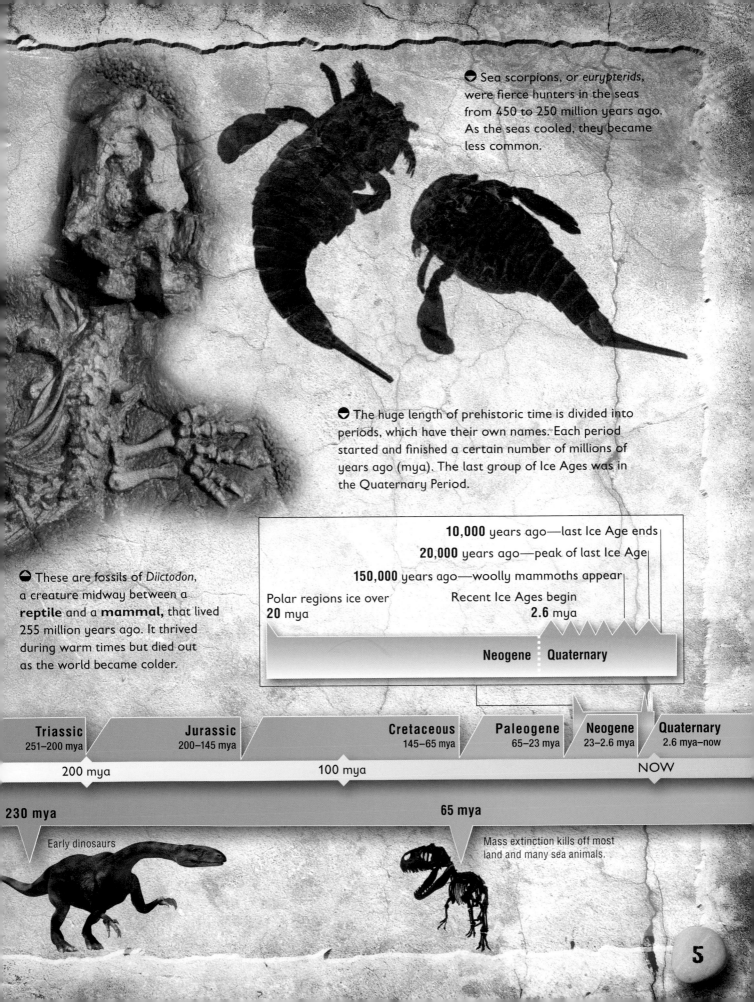

◐ Sea scorpions, or *eurypterids*, were fierce hunters in the seas from 450 to 250 million years ago. As the seas cooled, they became less common.

◐ The huge length of prehistoric time is divided into periods, which have their own names. Each period started and finished a certain number of millions of years ago (mya). The last group of Ice Ages was in the Quaternary Period.

◐ These are fossils of *Diictodon*, a creature midway between a **reptile** and a **mammal**, that lived 255 million years ago. It thrived during warm times but died out as the world became colder.

10,000 years ago—last Ice Age ends
20,000 years ago—peak of last Ice Age
150,000 years ago—woolly mammoths appear

Polar regions ice over
20 mya

Recent Ice Ages begin
2.6 mya

Neogene **Quaternary**

Triassic	**Jurassic**	**Cretaceous**	**Paleogene**	**Neogene**	**Quaternary**
251–200 mya	200–145 mya	145–65 mya	65–23 mya	23–2.6 mya	2.6 mya–now

200 mya   **100 mya**   **NOW**

230 mya   **65 mya**

Early dinosaurs

Mass extinction kills off most land and many sea animals.

RECENT ICE AGES

A series of about twenty Ice Ages began 2.5 million years ago. The last one finished only around 10,000 years ago.

During each of these Ice Ages, ice spread over much of the land and the sea in the northern half of the world, and over large areas of the southern half. After 40,000 years or more, a warmer period followed and most of the ice melted away.

Animals that were very different to those alive today lived during the Ice Ages. *Homotherium*, the scimitar cat, used its sword-like curved front teeth to slice up its victims, such as deer.

WILD!

In just one cave in Texas, North America, the remains of more than 30 *Homotherium* were found. The cave also contained remains of their food—more than 300 young mammoths!

WILD FILE

Homotherium

GROUP Mammals—cats

WHEN Five million to 10,000 years ago

FOOD Deer, wild cattle, elephants, mammoths, rhinos, horses

FOSSIL SITES Most northern lands, also North Africa

● Fossil sites

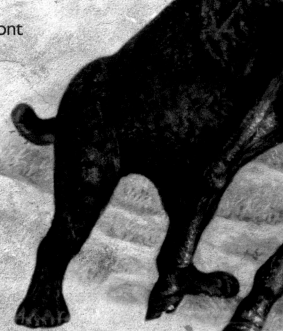

At the peak of the most recent Ice Age, much of North America and Northern Europe were completely covered by a thick sheet of ice. The lands to the south were much colder than they are today.

Homotherium may have hunted in groups to catch prey such as wild horses. The fierce cats clawed, jabbed, and stabbed the victim so it bled to death.

The World 20,000 Years Ago

Northern Ice Sheet

Europe

Asia

America

Africa

Australia

South American Ice Sheet

Australian Ice Sheet

HOW BIG?

Homotherium
Length 6.5 feet (2 meters)

KEEPING WARM

To keep warm in cold weather, you put on a coat. Some Ice Age animals grew their own warm coats—made of long fur or hair.

Only the animals called **mammals** have furry or woolly coats. One of the thickest coats belonged to the woolly **mammoth**, a type of elephant. Some of its hairs were more than 3 feet (1 meter) long. The woolly mammoth also had long, curving **tusks** to scrape away snow and reach its plant food.

The woolly rhinoceros also had a thick fur coat. Its front **nose horn** was more than 3 feet (1 meter) long.

WILD!

Woolly mammoths have been found deep-frozen in the ice of the far north. One, called "Baby Lubya," was just one month old when she died 40,000 years ago, in the far north of what is now Russia.

The woolly rhinoceros had two nose horns. It lived across the north of Europe and Asia. It was even larger than the biggest rhinoceros of today, the white rhino of Africa.

WILD FILE

Woolly mammoth

GROUP Mammals—elephants

WHEN 150,000 to 4,000 years ago

FOOD Grasses, leaves, roots

FOSSIL SITES Northern parts of North America, Europe, and Asia

● Fossil sites

The tusks of the woolly mammoth reached 16 feet (5 meters) in length. This mammoth had a lumpy top to the head and a big shoulder hump, but quite small ears.

HOW BIG?

Woolly mammoth
11.5 feet (3.5 meters) to the shoulder

CAVE DANGERS

When a freezing wind brings lots of snow, a cave offers welcome shelter. But during the Ice Age, many caves had huge fierce animals inside!

The cave bear was a massive cousin of today's grizzly bear. It probably stayed in its cave through the long winter, in a deep sleep called **hibernation**. In the summer it wandered the grasslands and woods, searching for all kinds of food.

Other Ice Age creatures that sheltered in caves included cave lions and cave hyenas. Some Ice Age caves were very crowded!

WILD!

Some caves contain the remains of more than 100 bears. They may have all died together during an extra cold winter. There were also bones of their prey, such as deer.

WILD FILE

Cave bear

GROUP Mammals – bears

WHEN One million to 27,000 years ago

FOOD Most foods – plant and animal

FOSSIL SITE Western and Northern Europe

● Fossil sites

HOW BIG?

Cave bear
10 feet (3 meters)
long

⬤ After months in their shelter, a mother cave bear and her young cubs look out at the spring sunshine. They are very hungry, and it's time to go outside for fresh air and food.

⬤ Cave paintings by ancient humans show that the cave lion probably had faint stripes, like a tiger. It hunted all kinds of creatures, including caribou (reindeer).

MASSIVE PLANT-EATERS

Some Ice Age animals roamed the snowy grasslands, while others wandered in the woods and forests. The giant deer probably did both.

The giant deer's body was only slightly bigger than the largest deer today, the moose. But its **antlers** were far bigger. They measured more than 11.5 feet (3.5 meters) across and were very heavy—they weighed more than you!

As with most deer, only the males grew antlers. They probably used their antlers to fight each other at **breeding time**, to take control of the **herd** of females.

WILD FILE

Giant deer

GROUP Mammals – deer

WHEN 400,000 to 8000 years ago

FOOD Grasses, leaves, shoots, fruit

FOSSIL SITES Northern parts of Europe and Asia

● Fossil sites

HOW BIG?

Giant deer
7.2 feet (2.2 meters)

● The giant deer is sometimes called the "Irish elk" because many of its remains are found in peat bogs in Ireland. But it also lived in many other places across Europe and Asia.

● *Toxodon* lived in South America during the recent Ice Ages. It looked like a mixture of rhinoceros and hippopotamus, and it fed on grasses and low-growing shrubs.

HUNTERS, HUNTED

There were many hunting animals during the Ice Ages, including fierce wolves and powerful big cats.

The dire wolf was one of the main Ice Age **predators.** It probably hunted in groups called packs.

What did these wolves eat? We know about Ice Age animals from their fossils, which are the remains of once-living things preserved in the rocks and turned to stone. Fossils of dire wolves have been found with fossils of their victims, which have ranged from horses and deer to camels, elephants, and even giant beavers!

As well as being a hunter, the dire wolf may have been a **scavenger.** Its strong jaws and teeth could crunch up the bits of dead animals left by other predators such as **saber-toothed ca**

HOW BIG?

Dire wolf
6.5 feet (2 meters)
nose-to-tail

WILD FILE

Dire wolf

GROUP Mammals—carnivores

WHEN 1.8 million to 11,000 years ago

FOOD Many creatures, from mice to elephants

FOSSIL SITES North and South America

● Fossil sites

CLOSE COUSINS

The dire wolf was bigger than today's gray wolf and had longer, stronger legs. Once the dire wolf pack started chasing a victim, there was no escape!

● *Hipparion* was a small type of horse that lived in America during the early Ice Ages of recent times. It was attacked by many predators including dire wolves and the huge, fierce, flightless bird *Titanis*.

AWAY FROM THE ICE

Even during the coldest Ice Ages, some parts of the world stayed fairly warm. Yet more strange giant creatures lived here.

While northern areas were gripped by ice, the middle of the world—called the tropics—and some southern areas, were ice-free. One of the biggest animals here was the giant ground sloth.

As huge as an elephant, the giant ground sloth *Megatherium* had long, sharp claws to dig up plant food. It also used these fearsome claws to defend itself against enemies such as dire wolves and saber-toothed cats.

HOW BIG?

Giant ground sloth
20 feet (6 meters) high

● *Hippidion* was a pony-sized horse that lived in South America at the same time as the giant ground sloth. It died out around 8,000 years ago, perhaps hunted to extinction by people.

Giant ground sloth

GROUP Mammals— sloths and armadillos

WHEN Five million to 10,000 years ago

FOOD Plants

FOSSIL SITES Central and South America

● Fossil sites

WILD!

Megatherium's tongue may have been more than 3 feet (1 meter) long! The giant ground sloth could probably rear up and run on its two back legs with a kind of very fast waddle.

◗ *Megatherium* probably stood on its two rear legs and leaned back on its strong tail, to reach the leaves high up in trees. It could pull branches to its mouth with its big front claws.

DWARFS AND PYGMIES

Many Ice Age animals were much bigger than their relatives of today. Yet some were much smaller!

During the Ice Ages there were dwarf or "pygmy" kinds of many animals. Most lived on small islands where there was limited food. The pygmy mammoth of islands off western North America was probably not much taller than you. It weighed less than one-tenth of its giant cousin on mainland America, the Columbian mammoth.

There were also mini-versions of woolly mammoths, elephants, camels, rhinos, and horses.

HOW BIG?

Pygmy mammoth
5 feet (1.5 meters) to shoulder

◑ There were several kinds of *Teleoceras*, a rhinoceros with short legs and a small horn. The dwarf kind lived in swampy areas, wading and swimming like a hippopotamus.

Pygmy mammoths probably descended from the much larger Columbian mammoth. They lived on the Channel Islands, off the coast of what is now California.

WILD FILE

Pygmy mammoth

GROUP Mammals – elephants

WHEN One million to 11,000 years ago

FOOD Grasses, leaves

FOSSIL SITES Western North America

● Fossil sites

WILD!

The dwarf woolly mammoths of Wrangel Island, off Northeast Asia, survived until less than 4000 years ago. The island is small and very cold and snowy for most of the year, with little food.

AMAZING AUSTRALIA

Australia, in the south of the world, did not freeze much during the Ice Ages. But it was far colder than today, and some of its animals grew to huge sizes.

The giant wombat was the biggest-ever pouched animal, or **marsupial**. It roamed the plains and woods of Australia, feeding on all kinds of plants.

The giant wombat was so massive that it had few enemies. Perhaps a very hungry marsupial lion might attack it. Or a big eagle could swoop down to carry off its baby.

CLOSE COUSINS

The biggest marsupial today is the red kangaroo. It weighs up to 200 pounds (90 kilograms)—30 times less than its ancient cousin, the giant wombat.

WILD FILE

Giant wombat

GROUP Mammals—marsupials
WHEN 1.6 million to 40,000 years ago
FOOD Plants
FOSSIL SITES Australia

Fossil sites

HOW BIG?

Giant wombat
Length 10 feet (3 meters)
nose-to-tail

◗ The marsupial lion was smaller than the African lions of today. But it was very strong with an extremely powerful bite, and could probably kill a giant kangaroo.

◗ The giant wombat looked similar to its living cousin, the hairy-nosed wombat, but with a bigger head and snout. Like other marsupials it carried its baby in a pouch. Many of these wombats died of thirst in **droughts**.

DEADLY CATS

Many kinds of big cats hunted during the Ice Ages. Some had teeth that were longer than carving knives, and just as sharp!

Smilodon was a saber-toothed cat from North and South America. It had a short tail, but very strong legs and paws, for catching big **prey**.

Smilodon's two main front teeth were up to 12 inches (30 centimeters) long. They were very sharp but quite thin. *Smilodon* probably used them to stab into its victim, or to slash its flesh and cause gaping wounds so the prey bled to death.

WILD FILE

Smilodon

GROUP	Mammals—cats
WHEN	1.5 million to 10,000 years ago
FOOD	Other animals, from rats to elephants
FOSSIL SITES	North and South America

● Fossil sites

● *Megantereon* was one of the most widespread of saber-toothed cats. Its fossils have been found all around the north of the world and in Africa—where it chased antelopes and gazelles.

CLOSE COUSINS

The American giant lion of the Ice Ages was even larger than today's African lion. It was almost as big and heavy as the largest type of *Smilodon*, which was called *Smilodon populator*.

● *Smilodon* could open its mouth very wide, ready to strike its prey as though cutting it with a big knife. It may have gone for the throat —to cut the blood vessels and breathing tube.

HOW BIG?

Smilodon
7.2 feet (2.2 meters) nose-to-tail

MAMMOTH SIZE

There are no mammoths alive today. But during the Ice Ages, several kinds of these huge beasts roamed various parts of the world.

One of the biggest was the Columbian mammoth. It was twice as heavy as most living elephants. Almost as massive was its close cousin, the American **mastodon**.

Many mammoths and mastodons have been preserved in natural **tar pits**. Other plant-eaters died here too, such as ground sloths, giant buffalo, camels, deer, and horses. Hunters were also killed, including dire wolves, saber-toothed cats, and American lions and cheetahs.

WILD FILE

Columbian mammoth

GROUP Mammals—elephants

WHEN 250,000 to 8,000 years ago

FOOD Grasses, fruits, and other plant parts

FOSSIL SITES North and Central America

● Fossil sites

HOW BIG?

Columbian mammoth
13 feet (4 meters) to the shoulder

The Columbian mammoth's curving tusks stretched as long as a family car! The great beast probably used them to dig up roots, to snap branches off trees, and to fight its enemies.

◑ A mammoth's tusks grew gradually over the years, so the oldest mammoths had the longest tusks. The Columbian mammoth probably lived to the age of 70 or 80 years.

◒ The American mastodon was a close cousin of the elephants and mammoths. It probably fed on leaves from trees and bushes.

ICE AGE PEOPLE

During the Ice Ages, not only animals braved the freezing winds and thick snow. There were also human beings—people much like us.

Two kinds of humans lived during the recent Ice Ages. First were the Neanderthal people. They made stone tools such as scrapers and spears, built shelters, lit fires, and made clothes from animal furs to keep warm.

Neanderthals died out 30,000 years ago. As the Ice Age began to fade, another type of human, called **Homo sapiens,** spread more widely. These were modern humans—just like you.

WILD!

Neanderthal people probably used blazing torches to drive mammoths over cliffs or into pits. Then they ate the mammoth meat, wore their furry skin, and carved their tusks into tools.

More than 15,000 years ago, people drew pictures of animals in caves, such as this early horse. These pictures show us what many **extinct** animals looked like.

WILD FILE

Neanderthal human

GROUP Mammals – **primates**

WHEN 250,000 to 32,000 years ago

FOOD Many foods, from nuts and berries to mammoth meat

FOSSIL SITES Europe and West Asia

● Fossil sites

HOW BIG?

Neanderthal human
5.4 feet
(1.65 meters)

◑ Neanderthal people looked very similar to us. But they were stronger, with more powerful muscles, wider noses, longer bodies, and shorter legs. They used many kinds of tools to kill and cut up the animals they hunted.

WILD GUIDE

Diictodon
Pronunciation
die-ick-toe-don

Meaning Two teeth

Group Mammal-like reptiles

Time Late Permian, 255 mya

Length 24 in (60 cm)

Weight 6 lbs (3 kg)

Hipparion
Pronunciation
hip-are-ee-on

Meaning Pony

Group Mammals—horses

Time Neogene to Quaternary,
12 million to 750,000 ya

Height 4.6 ft (1.4 m)

Weight 220 lbs (100 kg)

Pygmy Teleoceras
Pronunciation
tell-ee-oh-sare-ass

Meaning Distant horn

Group Mammals—rhinos

Time Neogene, 10 to 5 mya

Length 8.2 ft (2.5 m)

Weight 660 lbs (300 kg)

Homotherium
Pronunciation
hoe-moe-theer-ee-um

Meaning Man-eating beast

Group Mammals—cats

Time Neogene to Quaternary,
5 million to 10,000 ya

Length 6.5 ft (2 m)

Weight 400 lbs (180 kg)

Giant ground sloth
Megatherium
Pronunciation
meg-ah-theer-ee-um

Meaning Great beast

Group Mammals—sloths and armadillos

Time Neogene and Quaternary,
5 million to 10,000 ya

Length 26 ft (8 m)

Weight 5.6 t

Megantereon
Pronunciation
meg-ant-er-ee-on

Meaning Owen's big animal

Group Mammals—cats

Time Neogene and Quaternary,
4.5 million to 400,000 ya

Length 7.2 ft (2.2 m)

Weight 330 lbs (150 kg)

American mastodon
Mammut americanum
Pronunciation
mamm-oot ah-mare-ick-arn-um

Meaning Mastodon of America

Group Mammals—elephants

Time Neogene and Quaternary,
3.7 million to 10,000 ya

Height 10 ft (3 m)

Weight 7.7 t

Toxodon
Pronunciation
tocks-owe-don

Meaning Poison tooth

Group Mammals—hoofed mammals

Time Quaternary, 2.6 million to 15,000 ya

Length 9 ft (2.7 m)

Weight 1 t

WILD GUIDE

Elasmotherium

Pronunciation ee-laz-mow-theer-ee-um

Meaning Thin plate beast

Group Mammals— rhinos

Time Quaternary, 2.5 million to 130,000 ya

Length 20 ft (6 m)

Weight 7.7 t (7 t)

Smilodon

Pronunciation smile-oh-don

Meaning Chisel tooth

Group Mammals—cats

Time Quaternary, 1.8 million to 10,000 ya

Length 7.2 ft (2.2 m)

Weight 880 lbs (400 kg)

Hippidion

Pronunciation hip-id-ee-on

Meaning Little horse

Group Mammals—horses

Time Quaternary, 2 million to 8000 ya

Height 4.6 ft (1.4 m)

Weight 660 lbs (300 kg)

Giant wombat Diprotodon

Pronunciation dip-roe-toe-don

Meaning Two front teeth

Group Mammals—marsupials

Time Quaternary, 1.6 to 40,000 ya

Length 10 ft (3 m)

Weight 2.2 t (2 t)

Marsupial lion Thylacoleo

Pronunciation thigh-la-coe-leo

Meaning Pouched lion

Group Mammals—marsupials

Time Quaternary, 2 million to 40,000 ya

Length 6.5 ft (2 m)

Weight 265 lbs (120 kg)

Doedicurus

Pronunciation Doe-ed-i-cure-us

Meaning Pestle or hammer tail

Group Mammals—sloths and armadillos

Time Quaternary, 1.5 million to 12,000 ya

Length 13 ft (4 m)

Weight 2.2 t (2 t)

Dire wolf Canis dirus

Pronunciation kan-iss die-rus

Meaning Dreadful wolf

Group Mammals—wolves

Time Quaternary, 1.8 million to 10,000 ya

Length 6.5 ft (2 m)

Weight 176 lbs (80 kg)

Cave bear Ursus spelaeus

Pronunciation ur-suss spell-ee-us

Meaning Bear of the cave

Group Mammals—bears

Time Quaternary, 1 million to 27,000 ya

Length 10 ft (3 m)

Weight 1,100 lbs (500 kg)

WILD GUIDE

Pygmy mammoth
Mammuthus exilis

Pronunciation
mam-oo-thus ex-ill-iss

Meaning Removed mammoth

Group Mammals—elephants

When Neogene Period, 1 million to 11,000 ya

Height 5 ft (1.5 m)

Weight 1,985 lbs (900 kg)

Cave lion Panthera
Leo spelaea

Pronunciation
pan-theera lee-oh spell-ee-a

Meaning Lion of the cave

Group Mammals—cats

Time Quaternary, 700,000 to 10,000 ya

Length 10 ft (3 m)

Weight 440 lbs (200 kg)

Giant deer
Megaloceros giganteus

Pronunciation
mega-low-sare-oss jie-gan-tee-us

Meaning Gigantic big-horn

Group Mammals—deer

Time Quaternary, 400,000 to 8,000 ya

Length 13 ft (4 m)

Weight 1,100 lbs (500 kg)

Columbian mammoth
Mammuthus columbi

Pronunciation
mam-oo-thus ko-lum-bee

Meaning Mammoth of Columbia

Group Mammals—elephants

Time Quaternary, 250,000 to 8000 ya

Height 13 ft (4 m)

Weight 11 t (10 t)

Neanderthal human
Homo neanderthalensis

Pronunciation
Hoe-moe nee-an-dur-taal-en-sis

Meaning Person from Neander Valley

Group Mammals—primates

When Quaternary, 250,000 to 32,000 years ago

Height 5.4 ft (1.65 m)

Weight 200 lbs (90 kg)

Woolly mammoth
Mammuthus primigenius

Pronunciation
mam-oo-thus prim-ee-geen-ee-us

Meaning First-made mammoth

Group Mammals—elephants

Time Quaternary, 150,000 to less than 4000 ya

Length 23 ft (7 m)

Weight 8.8 t (8 t)

Woolly rhino
Coelodonta

Pronunciation
seel-owe-don-ta

Meaning Chamber tooth

Group Mammals—rhinos

Time Quaternary, 100,000 to 10,000 ya

Length 14 ft (4.4 m)

Weight 2.2 t (2 t)

Modern human
Homo sapiens

Pronunciation
hoe-moe sap-ee-ens

Meaning Wise person

Group Mammals—primates

Time Quaternary, 200,000 ya until now

Height 5.4 ft (1.65 m)

Weight 165 lbs (75 kg)

GLOSSARY

Antlers Large, hard, usually branched, horn-like parts growing from the top of a deer's head. Only male deer have antlers, apart from caribou or reindeer, the females of which have them too.

Breeding time When animals of the same kind get together to breed or produce young. For many creatures this happens at a certain time of year, often spring.

Drought A long time period of dryness, without rain or other forms of water.

Extinct Not existing any more. An animal is extinct when all of its kind have died out.

Herd A group of animals that live together.

Hibernation When certain kinds of animals go into a long, deep sleep, usually to avoid difficult conditions such as the cold of winter.

Homo sapiens "Wise human," the scientific name for all the people alive today on Earth.

Mammal An animal that has hair or fur and produces milk for its babies.

Mammoth A large animal with a long nose trunk and two big tusks, similar to and closely related to the elephant and mastodon. All mammoths have become extinct, or died out. Mammoths were bigger than mastodons, with longer tusks and different teeth.

Mastodon A large animal with a long nose trunk and two tusks, similar to and closely related to the elephant and mammoth. All mastodons have become extinct, or died out. Mastodons were smaller than mammoths, with shorter tusks and different teeth.

Marsupial A mammal whose babies grow and develop in a pocket-like pouch on their mother's front, or belly.

North and South Poles The places at the top and bottom of the Earth—the farthest north or south that you can go.

Nose horns Horns that grow on the nose or snout, like those on a rhinoceros, rather than on the top of the head.

Predator An animal that hunts and kills other creatures, the prey, for its food.

Prey A creature that is killed and eaten by another animal, the predator.

Primates A mammal group where most kinds have grasping hands and feet, big forward-facing eyes and a long tail, and live in trees. Primates include lemurs, bushbabies, monkeys, apes, and humans.

Reptile A scaly, usually cold-blooded animal, such as a lizard, snake, crocodile, turtle, or dinosaur.

Saber-toothed cats Cats with a pair of very long, curved, down-pointing teeth, shaped like the type of sword called a saber.

Scavengers Animals that feed on dead bodies killed by other creatures, rather than killing these themselves.

Snowball Earth A time when much of planet Earth became very cold, with lots of snow and ice. Living things survived in only a few warmer parts of the world.

Tusk A very big, long tooth that sticks out of the mouth. Many animals have tusks, including elephants, walrus, warthogs, as well as extinct mammoths and mastodons.

Tar pits Places where thick, sticky tar or oil oozes naturally over the surface of the ground, forming a kind of black pool or lake where animals can become trapped and sink in.

INDEX